I am delighted to recommend this booklet and the entire RZIM Critical Questions Series to you. Written in a popular style and engaging manner, these booklets are authored by many notable thinkers and respected scholars.

They are uniquely and specifically designed for those who have questions about—and even difficulties with—belief in God and the credibility of the Christian faith.

Christian believers, too, will greatly benefit from this series, which will serve as an important tool to present and defend their faith in the marketplace of ideas.

I am convinced that these remarkable booklets will not disappoint in their readability and in their persuasiveness for those honestly seeking answers to life's deepest questions and to the cultural confusion around us.

Ravi K. Zacharias

Can I Trust the Bible?

Defending the Bible's Reliability

Darrell L. Bock

Darrell L. Bock is Research Professor of New Testament Studies at Dallas Theological Seminary in Dallas, Texas. He also serves as Professor for Spiritual Development and Culture for the Seminary's Center for Christian Leadership. His special fields of study involve hermeneutics, the use of the Old Testament in the New, Luke-Acts, the historical Jesus, and Gospels studies. He is a graduate of the University of Texas (B.A.), Dallas Theological Seminary (Th.M.), and the University of Aberdeen (Ph.D.). His publications include an immense two-volume commentary on Luke (Baker), *Luke: The NIV Application Commentary* (Zondervan), *Luke* (The IVP New Testament Commentary), *Blasphemy and Exaltation in Judaism and the Final Examination of Jesus* (Baker)—a major monograph on Jesus' judicial examination before the Jewish leadership, *Proclamation From Prophecy and Pattern* (Sheffield). He has contributed to essays in *Bibliotheca Sacra, Journal of the Evangelical Theological Society*, and the *Bulletin for Biblical Research*. Various essays of his have been included in books such as *Introducing New Testament Interpretation* (Baker), *Jesus Under Fire* (Zondervan), and *Witness to the Gospel: A Theology of Acts* (Eerdmans). He has served as a translation consultant to *The Message* and to *The New Living Translation.* He is currently working on a life of Christ textbook for Baker. He is married to Sally and has two daughters and a son.

ISBN 1-930107-03-X

3 IS THE BIBLE TRUSTWORTHY IN ITS HISTORICAL CONTEXT?

Introduction

Ancient books always have a strange feel about them. Created somewhere in a dark and distant past, the world they describe is often filled with strange dress, unusual customs, a different way of expressing things—and a foreign way of living. There are no telephones, cassette recorders, cameras, or airplanes. Instead there are letters, conversations, horses, or other beasts of burden. E-mail is either by word of mouth or recorded on scraps of leather or paper made from reeds. Reading a book from the past is like taking a journey to another land. For all its timelessness, the Bible also has that distant feel to it. After all, it was written over two millennia ago. Its roots do go back to a different time and place. All of that distance raises questions about whether or not what I read really belongs only to such a distant world. Does the Bible really reflect what that world was like, much less what my world is like? So it is natural to ask the question if the Bible is really trustworthy in its content. That question is what we shall consider in this booklet.

Matters are not as foggy as the distance of a few thousand years might suggest. We know a lot about the Bible and how it was produced. In fact, we know far more about it that any other ancient book. To say that does not mean we know everything about its production, nor does it mean that every question we can ask has an answer. However, if we can speak clearly about other areas of ancient history, then we certainly can speak about the Bible's general trustworthiness.[1]

To cover the topic, we shall begin by noting how we got the books of the Bible. To assess the Bible, we have to know what is included in it and what is not. So we will briefly treat issues about what is called the "canon," those books that are included in Scripture.[2] Are any of the recent works that one hears about in the media or sees on the shelves of books on religion in book stores, like the Gospel of Thomas, worthy to be considered on a level with the four gospels? What do we do with the differences in the Old Testament listings?

Next we consider the roots of the Bible's testimony and sources, the role and character of memory in Jewish culture, and what does inspiration mean. Is inspiration like dictation? From a consideration of sources, we also have to ask questions about history itself. How does history "work"? How does history work when one is treating a series of events, where later events reveal the significance of former events? What choices do writers have about how they present history? What three approaches are often taken toward biblical history? What internal evidence does the Scripture give for how it has approached such questions? Who has the burden of proof in assessing a text? Does the text have to show it is trustworthy? Is the burden on the critic who questions the text? Or should it lie on the one making the claim either for or against the text? What can we say about accuracy? Does that include being able to chronologically map out every sequence? Is precision demanded or just general accuracy? All these questions treat issues tied to assessing the Bible's reliability. Three chapters will cover these questions, many of which treat key suppositions.

These suppositions indicate how we often approach the question before we have even looked at the biblical text.

Looking at historicity, it is beneficial to consider what the history of biblical study teaches us. Here we consider specific examples emerging from archaeology and other historical study. Were there things said with certainty about the Bible that now have been questioned by something discovered that reveals a new set of historical conclusions? This is a way of looking at the Bible from the outside.

Next, we will look in the Bible itself to see how it indicates some of these matters are handled. Some of the tougher cases will be assessed. Perhaps we cannot answer a specific kind of question we can raise about the Bible because we have asked a question it does not seek to answer. Perhaps there is no answer because we do not yet possess enough outside information. This discussion will also give us a glance at how the Bible actually works. We also shall consider the issue of miracles through discussing two of the Bible's great miracles, the exodus and the resurrection. The premise that emerges from these two central events is that if the exodus and resurrection are defensible, so are miracles as a category.

After this overview of the key issues, we will be able to tackle anew our question about whether a book as ancient as the Bible can be shown to be historically trustworthy. Can the mirror it shines on past events be trusted? Then we will be in a better position to discuss the importance of what we have found. If there is the possibility that God has spoken through this text and has participated in the history it records, then the answers to our question are not a mere academic exercise. Our journey back into these seemingly foreign, ancient times may be a real opportunity to see more clearly who we are and were created to be.

THE CANON:

The Books of the Bible Have Been Recognized As Such for Hundreds of Years.

Factor 1

The term "canon" means a "measuring reed" and refers to a standard that is applied to some topic. When biblical books are described as the canon, they are identified as those books that the church has for centuries looked to as revealing God's way and will, those works inspired by God. The books contained in the Bible were written over a period of about fifteen hundred years, up through the first century AD. The New Testament canon contains twenty-seven books. Once it was finalized in the mid-fourth century, it has never been challenged—until recently. Discussion has existed about the inclusion/exclusion of some Old Testament books known today as the Apocrypha or the Deutero-canonicals. However, the thirty-nine books of the Old Testament, excluding the Apocrypha, have been recognized as canonical in Judaism almost since the time of Christ. The first century Jewish historian Josephus tells us that there are not "an innumerable multitude of books among us, disagreeing and contradicting one another [as the Greeks have], but only twenty-two books, which contain the records of past times" (*Against Apion* 1.38). He then names the five books of Moses, thirteen prophets, and four books of hymns and precepts alluding to among others, Psalms and Proverbs. Josephus' twenty two books follows the Jewish divisions of the Old Testament: *Torah*, *Prophets* (including the historical books and including the twelve prophets as a group), and *Writings*.[3] Qumran texts also attest to this basic division with the expression "the book of Moses, the words of the prophets and of David (4QMMT Frags. 7-8, 10). Only church disputes of the Reformation and Counter-Reformation periods led to the adoption of the Apocrypha by Catholics as Scripture. All of this raises the question about whether the books of the Bible were chosen for polemical reasons or whether their inclusion really was the product of a careful process.

When it comes to what we call the Old Testament, the process of recognition of sacred books was pretty much complete by the time of Christ. The initial message of the first Christians combined a message about what Jesus said and did with what was written in "the Scripture." In effect, the earliest Christians accepted the sacred books of Judaism as their Scripture. The books we now possess were consistently named as Scripture with only a few books being disputed now and then as to whether they should be included (Esther, Proverbs, Song of Solomon, Ecclesiastes, Ezekiel).[4] The rule seems to have been—*if a book is really in doubt, leave it out.* Still a few other works, mostly some of the key works in the Apocrypha, did show up in ancient Jewish collections with scriptural books. They were closely tied to Scripture because they either treated the key historical period associated with recent Israelite independence tied to the Maccabees or because the given work contained Jewish wisdom that was viewed as valuable. However, when the Hebrew Scriptures were named in a list, those works tended to be absent. Those additional works were appreciated as instructive and worthy of study, much like we might appreciate a good book that has lots of information and wisdom, but they were not regarded as possessing the same value and authority as those books that were regarded as Scripture.

Interestingly, the process of recognition tied to the New Testament books was more complicated and yet yielded complete agreement when the process was finalized. There is no doubt that some of the catalyst for identifying the New Testament canon was motivated by disputes that broke out concerning Christian teaching in the early centuries after the birth of the new faith. The dispute with Marcion around AD 140 seems to have really given impetus to this effort to identify the received books. After all, some Christian subgroups and fringe groups wrote their own documents, claiming to possess authority for all the church. In addition, the reading of sacred texts as a part of worship required that those books be identified. A process of sorting out the valuable from the spurious began, and the church proceeded carefully and took a few centuries to settle on the matter. What is crucial to appreciate here is that the church *did not pick the books of the canon, but undertook a process to recognize them. They received only those books they regarded as giving evidence of divine authority.*

In fact, some lists, like the *Muratorian Canon* (around the late second century) listed works like the *Shepherd of Hermas* as "worthy to be read" while distinguishing it from the canonical books. Thus by the end of the second century, a concept of the need to identify the inspired books was already established. Among the New Testament books that were disputed were: 2 Peter, 2 and 3 John, James, Jude, and Revelation. *Shepherd*, the Epistle of Barnabas, the Apocalypse of Peter, the Didache (pronounced *di-dä-kay)*, the Gospel according to the Hebrews, and 1 and 2 Clement sometimes appeared in early groupings. The *Gospel of Thomas*, often discussed by some today as a fifth gospel, *never* shows up in these lists. This question of which books were to be received was sorted out over the next few centuries.

However, two collections emerged almost immediately: the fourfold gospel collection and a collection of Pauline epistles. Our evidence is that by early in the second century the gospels had already been received. They were popular enough that by AD 170 Tatian put them together in a harmony. In AD 180, Irenaeus speaks of a fourfold gospel as if it were a given.[5] So the core of the New Testament was identified very early on.

Several *tests* emerged for considering a text as worthy. Among them was *a connection to the apostolic roots of the church*, which would tie the teaching to the most important early disciples, enhancing the given book's claim to be credible. This did not mean that an apostle had to be the author. It did mean that the work had to have contact with an apostolic source. So Mark was not an apostle, but his gospel was closely associated with the preaching of Peter.[6] Luke (who also wrote Acts) was associated with Paul in ministry and had contact with other apostles. This criterion excluded works that were later in origin, which prevented the "production" of Scripture after the second generation after Christ. The New Testament should be and was rooted in the earliest history of the church.

Another test was *the usefulness of the work across the church, both geographically and across time*. Scripture should not give evidence of being "sectarian." Interestingly, one of the more disputed books in this process was Revelation, as its visions of the end were so difficult to understand that there was concern if it really was a work that built up the church. In the end, it was the apostolic roots of the work in John that carried the day, as difficulty of content was not held to deny its usefulness.

Other less controversial works were produced for the instruction of believers. Some of these were initially treated similarly to Scripture. Works like the Epistle to Barnabas and the Didache were cited by some in the early period as if they were Scripture. However, along with usefulness across the church, there came a sense about whether a work continued to be appreciated as time had passed. In this way, they could be distinguished as not equal to works that were less disputed. Thus, these later works, though they continued to be read and studied as valuable, were not ultimately ranked in the exclusive category of canon. Rather they became associated with a collection that came to be known as the Apostolic Fathers.[7]

In sum, the canon emerged through a long and careful process of reflection in which the church, considering what she believed and what these books taught, embraced some as reflective of her faith in a way that caused her to recognize, receive, and affirm their inspiration. By the end of the second century, the core of what became the New Testament was recognized. Many other works continued to be assessed in the next two centuries that followed. The list of recognized books, once it emerged, has since served as the New Testament. For centuries, this grouping was accepted as reflecting the content of the New Testament.

Recently, there have been some who have treated the selection of the New Testament canon as primarily a political and sociological process in which the "orthodox" won simply because they held the power. The argument goes that Christianity was far more diverse than this "controlled" view of the church's history admits. In fact, it is only the changes brought about in the aftermath of the Enlightenment, as well as the discovery of some of the older works of these fringe groups, that has opened up this discussion in recent times. There is an element of truth in the claim that those who finalized the process of canonical recognition were those who held power in the church. However, it also is the case that all the fringe works brought forward never had the kind of wide circulation and acceptance among the bulk of believers that commended these works as canon.

Works that today have been hailed as new examples of ancient Scripture, like the second century Gospel of Thomas, belong in this class and surely are not to be seen as canonical. First, Thomas reflects a Gnosticism that some in the early church became intrigued with, but that the church came to reject as deficient. Gnosticism basically argued against the value of the material world and for the primacy of spiritual forms. This meant for Gnostics that Jesus had a spiritual form only, not a real physical body, nor was he truly human. If he walked on a beach, one could see him but he would leave no footprints. Second, the idea that a book equal to scriptural status should be unused in the church for centuries violates the idea that if a work is canonical, it will have had a wide circulation in the community of faith that embraces its teaching.

So our first point is that the Bible we have is the Bible we should assess. The canon and the deliberate process of recognition it represents identifies for us those books that we need to consider when we ask if the Bible is trustworthy. We can ask the question with confidence knowing which books we should examine.

ASSUMPTIONS ABOUT RELIABILITY:

The Bible's Claim To Be a Divine Book Also Involves Acknowledged Human Dimensions — The Use of Trustworthy Sources and the Ability To Pass on Such Information in a Structured, Stable Way.

Factor 2

The Bible is a book both like other books and unlike them. Within its pages there is the acknowledgement that sources of various types stand behind its material. This makes the Bible sound like any book. Luke's admission of sources (Luke 1:1-4) and the fact that he sought to check them are an indication that the writers tried to exercise care in how they presented the text.[8] John's gospel makes even stronger source claims with respect to his story, grounding it in his own witness testimony (John 21:24: "This is the disciple who is bearing witness to these things"). The verse also includes the additional note by others vouching for the account's trustworthiness (John 21:24).[9] Certain texts also make claims with regard to how writers would be able to recall certain events. For example, there is Jesus' promise of the Spirit as a means by which what Jesus taught would be brought to memory later for Jesus' closest disciples (John 14:14:25-26). Some of these claims look like things we recognize about how books are written, while other elements do not.

So the concept of inspiration entails a claim that God has involved himself in the process of producing Scripture. God speaks through the human writers. However, the Bible also discusses how this claim for a divine role works. The divine superintention of the Bible's content does not mean that God is dictating the words of Scripture, but that he has motivated its content down to the wording of its message (2 Timothy 3:16-17). 2 Peter 1:20-21 speaks of men being borne along by the Spirit who spoke from God. Like the wind drives a boat through its sail, God gives the Scripture its initiative, path, and direction; but there still is a human author who mans the helm. Anyone reading the Bible can see the variety of styles that mark its pages. To argue that the Bible is a book inspired by God does not dismiss the human elements that make up the book.[10] Still it is one thing to make claims, yet another to see if there are reasons to suggest that those claims should be embraced.

One of the obstacles people sometimes raise about the Bible's credibility is that so much time has passed from the events it describes to their recording. Is there not a great potential for distorting the story as it passes down from generation to generation until it is recorded? Sometimes this can even grow into an assumption that such a passage of time *must* have led to distortion in the tradition. This issue strikes at the heart of the human dimensions of the Bible. What about the sources of its message and the nature of the traditions that are tied to that message?

What, then, can one say about the sources of Scripture? In the case of the texts surrounding Jesus, the role of eyewitnesses as being at the root of the tradition is strong. Luke himself speaks about how those who began to circulate the stories about Jesus, were eyewitnesses and ministers of the Word (Luke 1:2). As we noted, he claimed to be careful about how his work was done. Many writers of the Bible, especially in the New Testament, were people at the events described or people who had access to others who were there.

For Mark's gospel, tradition long held that what is present are the memoirs of Peter's preaching. Matthew has roots in the work of the apostle by that name. John has similar apostolic roots.[11] Remember that, for the New Testament, an apostolic association is important to establishing the account's inclusion in the canon. This standard was because of a concern about the account's credibility. For most of the New Testament books, such associations are accepted by most scholars as part of their roots. Many of these works were written within the lifetime of participants in these events. The distance between event and recording is not great — less than a lifetime, a small distance of time by ancient standards. Many other great works of ancient history involve a separation time of centuries from the events. For example, the first century Roman historians Livy and Dionysius of Halicarnassus were centuries removed from many of the events they chronicled as opposed to decades away as is the case for the New Testament.

However, this connection to actual witnesses is not the case with all the books of the Bible, perhaps even much of it. Some of its contents were passed on by oral tradition or through sources. Occasionally, such sources are named (2 Kings 15:26, 31). In other cases, we do not know what the exact sources of information were. This makes exact corroboration hard to establish, but *that is a fact for virtually all the events we work with from ancient history, many of which we accept without any parallel accounts.*

We do know that within Judaism there existed the ability to pass on things with care from one generation to the next. This does not mean that one necessarily passed on the contents word for word, but it does mean that the recounting of events was done with care for the core of the story. That some variation in telling an event took place is obvious by comparing the gospels' accounts or

Samuel-Kings-Chronicles to one another. One can see the same trend in comparing rabbinical parallel accounts to one another. What we also see in general is *a recognizable core* to the account.[12]

That such passing on of a text or an account could be exact is indicated in the history of the Old Testament text. For years our oldest manuscripts of the Old Testament came from the tenth century AD (known as the Masoretic text). Claims were made that the text was in a terrific degree of oral flux with things added to or subtracted from the text on a regular basis. When the Dead Sea Scrolls were discovered in the 1940s, such theories could be tested with actual documents that leapt over a thousand years of transmission history, as the documents found in these caves were that much older than what we had previously. The copies of Isaiah found at the caves of Qumran were virtual matches for their thousand year younger descendants.[13] The text tradition for the Hebrew text had remained stable for a millennium. Again, the point is not to argue that there are never variations in the text or that every copy was perfect, for we know that is not the case. But what can be shown is that the text of the Old Testament was passed on with a stability that speaks credibly for the traditional process.

Judaism, and the Christianity that grew out of it, was a culture of memory, where the basic elements of an account were retained. People memorized long liturgical prayers and more often than not worked from memory rather than from a written page. Anyone who has read children's book again and again to their child knows that the mind is capable of absorbing vast amounts of wording and retaining it. My daughters, when they were three, used to delight in finishing the sentences of their favorite stories. For ancient Jews working orally was the norm, not the exception. It is perhaps hard for us as modern people so used to the written word to appreciate what it was like to habitually work with the oral word.

In later chapters, we shall consider how the variation within tradition worked and what it means for trustworthiness, but our basic point here is that when it came to tradition Jewish culture cared about, that tradition gives evidence of being fairly stable. For all the attention that many pay to the differences between accounts within the Bible, those portions that overlap show the same fundamental story. Often at their most basic levels, they make the same basic points.

In addition, there are some traces of processes that indicate how those who watched over the tradition could carefully pass events on from one era to the next. In some cases we can identify the "forms" of these stories, that is, their basic genre structure which stories of a similar type tended to possess so that they could be passed on and remembered. For example, a miracle account in the gospels often gives

(a) a setting and then

(b) describes the distress or condition of the person seeking healing.

Next comes

(c) the approach to Jesus with some kind of exchange leading Jesus to speak or act.

The next detail

(d) usually describes the evidence that a healing has taken place.

Finally, there appears

(e) the reaction from the one healed or the crowd.

Once one recognizes the form in which miracle accounts were passed on, then one can appreciate how their basic structure could be passed on and retained. Now it is true that form does not guarantee accuracy. It would be possible for someone to create a story and have it mimic the structure. However, what the presence of form does suggest is that when stories were passed on, they took on a form that made retaining the basic story manageable.

Corroborating the trustworthiness of ancient events is hard to do. In later chapters we shall return to this question. For now my basic point is that the nature of Jewish and early Christian culture made the potential retention of such events possible.

One corollary point also belongs here. We are confident that the text of the Bible we work with today basically reflects the text as it was produced. This is certainly the case with New Testament, which has far better manuscript evidence for its wording than any other ancient document.[14] Where most ancient works we study in the classics, such as Plato, Herodotus and Aristophanes, have from a few to twenty manuscripts (many have only one), the New Testament has about 5,400 Greek manuscripts that we can compare to determine the wording, not to mention the over 8,000 ancient Latin manuscripts.[15] These manuscripts show how fundamentally stable the reproduction of the text was over hundreds of years in a time before Xerox machines. We do not have the treasury of evidence for the Old Testament text that we do for the New. However, it also is among the best-attested documents of the ancient world.

So the text we have of the Bible gives good evidence of being the text that was given. In addition, the process of passing on tradition had in place methods by which events could be faithfully passed on. All these observations do is set the table for the rest of the discussion, knowing that the passing of much time between the event and its recording need not be an obstacle for trustworthiness.

ASSUMPTIONS ABOUT RELIABILITY:

Discussing and Assessing Reliability Means Understanding and Appreciating the Complex Nature of What We Call History

Factor 3

So what about the differences in the Bible? Does not the Bible possess so many differences that it becomes hard to accept its trustworthiness? Here is another assumption Bible readers often make: *difference = contradiction, error, or lack of credibility*. In fact, I recently watched a nationally televised special on the life of Jesus. It perpetuated this error by repeatedly appealing to some scholars and historians for whom *difference = error*. Before we make such a judgment, it would be well to pause and consider how complex the notion of history is, especially when it comes to assembling the details that make it up.

The assessment of historicity is a complex process. First of all, there is *the issue of the differing perspectives from which events can be viewed, all of which can have historical merit.* I like to ask people what the original name was of the international conflict that emerged in the second decade of the twentieth century. Only a few realize that it was initially called "The Great War" or the "War to End All Wars." Both names expressed the scope of the conflict, which was unprecedented up to that time. The name this conflict is known by today is "The First World War," a name it could not have until the Second World War took place. Now whether one refers to this event by its original name, The Great War, or by its alternative, The Second World War, one is looking at the same set of historical events. In history, events have some element of dynamic flow, for their impact and meaning often become clear not from the event itself, but from the subsequent impact of the event. Thus in writing history, one can write from a perspective that is like the way the event was experienced and/or from a perspective that is aware of its subsequent impact. Each approach is historical but takes on the story with a narrower or larger frame of reference in mind. As such, differing perspectives and details can emerge as each perspective impacts which details are picked up.

For example, a well-known difference in the gospels exists in the healing of the centurion's slave accounts between Matthew and Luke. In Matthew 8:6-9, the centurion asks Jesus directly to heal his slave, while in Luke 7:3-8 Jewish emissaries make the request and the centurion is never physically present before Jesus. One option is simply to say the accounts are in hopeless contradiction, using the formula that difference = error. However, another option is to realize that in that culture, speaking to a commissioned representative is like speaking to the person being represented. An example in our culture is when the White House press secretary speaks. What is important is not especially who he is but that he speaks for the president. Ancient culture was similar. Now for Matthew, who is writing to a Jewish audience about Jewish issues, his perspective is focused simply on the fact that Jesus did reach out to Gentiles. These Gentiles, as represented by the centurion, showed exceptional faith that excelled most of the Jewish response. His perspective was limited to concerns tied to Israel. In contrast, Luke's gospel was for a mixed audience. It was probably written to a God-fearer, a Gentile who found himself in what was originally a Jewish movement. Part of Luke's concern was no doubt fueled in part by the passage of time and the move of the church into Gentile regions. What this event could underscore was not only that Gentiles had contact with Jesus but that a relationship had emerged between Gentiles and Jews as a result. For Luke the extra detail of Jewish elders being commissioned to speak on behalf of the Gentile spoke to this racial harmony that was a part of the event. Matthew, writing with Jewish concerns as primary, was not interested in this additional detail. Now the details told in the accounts do differ, but not because of error, but because of a difference of perspective which has led to different details surfacing because of the slightly different historical angles each writer has undertaken.

In other words, history, especially when dealing with multiple sources, is not one-dimensional with only one set of possible facts to present. The portrayal of history is framed by what concerns drive the choice of details presented. Many differences between the gospels, which some reject on the simplistic difference = error formula, are more likely the product of the fact that different writers present different concerns. These distinct concerns lead them to highlight different points of a history that is larger than any one account.

In fact, history can be read in one of three different ways.[16] One is a kind of *naïve positivism: What is in an account is what happened.* What I see and what I judge it to be is what it is. Read it as it is presented on the page. Do not ask questions. What you see is what was. So for example, when Jesus was baptized and the voice from heaven spoke, it must have been a public event where all heard the voice. Many great paintings of the Western world depict the event in this way. The *problem* with such a reading is that when multiple accounts appear and different details emerge, then there becomes a question of how the differing accounts relate. A closer look shows us that Mark 1:11 has the voice address Jesus in the second person ("you") and notes that only Jesus saw the heaven open and the dove descend. As Mark describes the event, it is a private experience for Jesus. Only John 1:30-34 makes us aware that John the Baptist also saw the event. For some, these differences bring doubt and raise questions. The easiest option is to reject positivism and simply throw up one's hands and say, "There is an error here; difference must equal error." This is what skeptics do, which is ironic for their approach to reading the text is often as simplistic as the "literalists" they criticize for being naïve, credulous readers. Another response is simply always to harmonize, put all the facts together and assert everything is so, even in a way that adds details not in any single description. So, for example, some try to protect the difference in the account of Peter's three denials by arguing that there were six.(because of the variety of participants noted) It may just be that as the denials proceeded, *more than three people* challenged Peter though different accounts note only *some* of those participants. One must reckon with selectivity between these texts as well. Or some suggest that at the temptations there were two sets of three temptations because the order differ between the accounts in Matthew 4:1-11 and Luke 4:1-13. Now my point is not that such responses in making sense of the material are automatically wrong or impossible but that always to use one approach or the other is likely to be wrong in some individual cases. Positivism ignores engaging history in its complexity.

On the other end of the spectrum is a skeptical approach, what is known as *"phenomenalism."* Here *we only accept what our senses tell us, the way things appear to us, what the "phenomena" of our own lives and world tell us.* The approach was a reaction to naïve positivism and was a product of the Enlightenment. On top of this worldview comes an element that also argues that the phenomena I experience are a matter of my own perception and judgment only. So the approach is clothed with an air of neutrality and the appearance of humility, while in fact a worldview is still assertively present. As "it seems to me" becomes a way of walling off difficult questions that try to get at whether there really are "facts" out there to appreciate, even if those facts may be more complex than a positivist might acknowledge. It is true that all of us tend to see things from our own perspective, but this does not close us off from being able to learn or see through the eyes of others. Nor should we be so confident that what we know and see is all there is to be known and seen. Phenomenalism possesses an arrogance that walls off the possibility of God speaking virtually by definition. When our senses and our own perspective become the sole arbiter of all we can know, then we have cut ourselves off from being able to learn about those elements of living that are spiritually rooted. In addition, such a position is self-refuting because it claims to know *really* or *factually* that *appearance* is all we have access to. In reality the claim that phenomena are all we know is just as much a claim outside the observation of phenomena as the positivistic view it claims to refute.

A third option is what we might call *"critical realism."*[17] Realism means *there are things outside myself and my perception that are there and are knowable.* Included in this are realities about history. However, this view also *recognizes the reality and function of differing perspectives.* This recognition of differing perspectives is critical when multiple sources are at work. When more data come or when multiple sources exist, there is an engagement with the data in such a way that the judgment and syntheses made of *all* the sources may not look exactly like any *one* of those sources. Critical realism seeks to relate all the data to the whole of the topic. It recognizes that the differing accounts may treat distinct details or angles of the story, making a fresh synthesis necessary to begin to get at the whole event. Such critical realism also understands that any one account of events, though it may be accurate or erroneous, is not exhaustive. As such, any account can be supplemented by another account of the same set of events, possibly even presenting the details in ways that differ from the first account.

Let's make all of this definitional discussion concrete with an example. We have two accounts of Jesus' birth material. These accounts differ enough that the difference = error game is often played with this material. Others more modestly say, we cannot know what took place, but again, the differences create a hesitation to embrace the accounts with confidence. A careful reading of the text, however, shows that *Luke* tells the account with *Mary* in mind, while *Matthew* focuses on *Joseph's perspective*. Now there is nothing inherently contradictory about these two perspectives, one a husband's and the other a wife's. In addition, anyone who has been married knows that when couples tell stories, the details they work with and what struck each of them about a shared experience differ. Often both spouses have varying, though legitimate, insights on the event in question. The story is richer when both versions are set forth.

So here Matthew is concerned in part to explain how Joseph, who knew where babies come from, decided to marry a women who, it had appeared, had conceived a child out of wedlock. Only the unusual circumstances of the birth permitted the pious prospective husband to finalize the marriage. Skeptics claim the story is created to give Jesus an air of "divinity" like other ancient greats. This story, however, is not told like the ancient versions. These accounts are modest and less sexually oriented. Where Claudias is claimed to have been conceived through a god in the form of a snake having intercourse with his mother, Jesus is the product of the mere Word of God and the work of his Spirit.[18] Moreover, consider the resulting alternative that this Roman parallel view requires, namely that Jesus really was born out of wedlock. Would the church really create such a potentially embarrassing story about its leader (i.e., about Joseph's doubt), if Jesus' birth had really been illegitimate? Would the "roots" of a "holy" messiah for a sacred calling have such a questionable start in reality? Could Jesus have ever really been a candidate for such a role if his real origin was so morally suspect? If the church were really just creating stories to fit the culture, then why not have the "divine" birth take place without the additional embarrassment of it being in a non-wedded context? Why not have the timing of it be that Mary as a virgin was with child in the context of the natural timing her marriage with Joseph? In other words after nine months with Joseph, the child is born. Once we start fabricating scenarios for the historical details as skeptics do, questions really multiply. The alternative looks less and less like a credible solution.

Luke lacks any of this controversy. He solely seeks to explain the sheer joy and surprise the mother had in going though this experience. Matthew, seeing the problems the birth raised, sees the glass half empty and explains how the scene was not as bad as it looked. Luke, captivated by the sheer experience and Mary's joy, sees the glass half full and presents the emotion of her involvement. The fact that Luke details a journey to Bethlehem to partake in a census, while Matthew simply details the birth is a simple case of each writer picking different details to fill out the description of the event.

The use of differing, but complementary perspectives is the way the Bible often works–particularily in the gospels with its parallel accounts.[19] Differing angles on the account complement and enrich the story. That can take place without the accounts contradicting each other.

Writing history is inevitably a matter of selection and choice in terms of the details presented. No account—no matter how good—tells everything. Perspective is always present—not just facts—because what is included and excluded is in part related to why and with what concerns the story is being told. In making this point, we are not arguing that to have a point of view is inevitably to distort the history. Some critics suggest that because believers wrote the books of the Bible, the facts are inevitably distorted. It is more accurate to say that history, when it is presented within an account's point of view, may not be the only angle to that history or the only way the events were perceived and assessed. Historically assessing an account's trustworthiness does not mean other points of view are excluded or irrelevant. Nor does it mean that other accounts, if found, may not add to the picture, whether they come from within the same camp or outside of it. Trustworthiness simply affirms that the assessed account is a credible portrayal of what took place—not that it is the only way the events in question were seen.

Another way to say this is that presenting history is not an exhaustive enterprise. One can have historical trustworthiness without giving every detail about an event. Other sources to that event can add to what we know about it without necessarily matching in every particular. Choices made in terms of what perspective is used to tell the story impact what is presented. Sometimes a more *summarizing* style is adopted in covering events – a choice that may give an account an appearance of inaccuracy when laid next to a more detailed account.

Again, let us give some examples. If we set the dialogue of certain scenes involving the same event next to one another in the Bible we will note some variation in wording. Skeptics often point to these as showing untrustworthiness. For them difference = either error or uncertainty. For example, take the account of Jesus' baptism by John the Baptist, which was already noted earlier. Did the voice from heaven say to Jesus, "*this* is my beloved Son," as Matthew 3:17 has it? Or did the voice utter, "*You* are my beloved Son," as Mark 1:11 and Luke 3:33 have it? One option (the positivistic approach) is to argue both were said and each author picked one example. Another option ("critical realism") is to argue that one set of gospel writers *quoted* (Mark, Luke), while the other *summarized* its significance (Matthew). In other words, the voice spoke to Jesus, addressing him as "you," but the other gospel writer gave the real historical significance of the event, the presentation of "this one" as the Son. Either option results in a conclusion where difference ≠ error. Now one might discuss which of these options is better or more likely. I prefer the summarizing option for this example. Regardless of which option is taken, note that at its most basic level the story is the same, despite the differences. At John's baptism a heavenly voice endorsed Jesus and identified him as Son. On that all the accounts agree. While we cannot be absolutely certain of how the details of the wording worked, we can see the basic point that all the accounts share. The Bible has historical trustworthiness in this sense. Once one takes into account how history works, the data from all the texts, and the complexity of presenting it, especially in multiple accounts, then one can begin to appreciate not only that the Bible is *trustworthy*, but that the study of the differences may well *enrich* that account.

We have tended to concentrate on problems. Let's look at a positive example. A few years ago, I spent a year in Germany doing research on the Jewish examination of Jesus that led to his death. I considered two themes: what Jews considered blasphemy to be and what they believed about exalted figures (people who get to go into God's presence in heaven for any reason). These two themes clash at the Jewish examination of Jesus, for Jesus claimed that he soon would be at God's side in heaven with judgment authority, while the leadership thought that claim was blasphemy. Thus, the scene is an important one in the gospels.

My year of research showed me that this account cohered nicely with what we know about blasphemy and exaltation in Judaism. The dialogue made "cultural sense" both from the standpoint of the leadership and from Jesus' claims.[20] What Jesus argued he would do had elements of precedent in Jewish hope for great figures like Moses and Enoch, even though Jesus' claims were slightly more unique.[21] How the Jews reacted fit nicely for a group that rejected Jesus' claim that he would go directly into God's presence. The whole scene ultimately revolves around Jesus' claims to uniquely represent God. The event looks trustworthy at its conceptual core.

Sometimes the objection is made that the details of this scene differ between the accounts. However, those differences reflect different choices made from a larger pool of information about an event that ran through an entire late evening and early morning.

Sometimes it is argued that the testimony is fabricated because there were no disciples present to be witnesses.

Such a claim ignores three key facts.

(1) Some members of the council, like Joseph of Arimathea, were there at the events or had access to those who were. Joseph as a Jesus-sympathizer could have easily passed on his understanding of the scene.

(2) People like the old persecutor Paul would have had access to the leadership and would have known the story from within.

(3) The execution of a key public figure like Jesus and the discussion it would have produced in a tight community like Jerusalem means that the reasons for his execution would have circulated as part of the public debate that surfaced when the disciples starting preaching about the resurrected Jesus. The leadership would not have been shy in explaining how they, in their view, had been faithful stewards as leaders of the Jewish faith to protect it from one making exaggerated claims. One can think of how political word spreads today when insider information gets leaked to the news media. Such important information in the midst of a dispute tends to surface in the public debate.

All of this suggests that the claim for credibility of this key scene is excellent. It is the trustworthiness of these key points of any story that are so important to appreciate about the Bible's credibility. If these key points reflect what took place and why, then the message of the Bible takes on ultimate importance. So we argue that an appreciation of the differing perspectives that emerge from the Bible and its parallel portraits enhances its portrayal of history. The differences are not evidence of error, but of the complexity of how good history gets effectively told.

ASSUMPTIONS ABOUT RELIABILITY:

Who Bears the Burden of Proof for Claims about Historicity?

Factor 4

Corroborating events that took place thousands of years ago is not easy work. The fact is that for most of ancient history, we know only the barest of outlines of what took place. Our sources are few. Many events we know about only though one source. Sorting out what is claimed from what took place is not always easy. This situation means that there is much discussion about the burden of proof when it comes to a document's claims.[22]

There are really three options on the burden of proof: a document must prove its credibility, one must accept the document's claim unless there is good reason to think otherwise, or the burden is on the historian to present the case for or against the document. In the case of the well-known Jesus Seminar, which has rejected much of the historicity of the gospels, several participants stated that the text was assumed *inauthentic*, so one had to prove its *authenticity*. This approach immediately skewed their results. Any singly-attested detail (rather than a multiply-attested passage) was immediately excluded as uncorroborated. The effect of such a standard applied to ancient sources outside the Bible would mean there is much of ancient history that we do not know, because so many events are singly-attested.[23] Though corroboration is valuable when it is available, it often fails as an absolute standard in working with ancient sources. It is often unrealistic to expect the presence of corroborative evidence. Most ancient historians in fields outside of biblical studies prefer to operate and in fact *must* operate with a standard that allows for singly-attested events.[24]

More plausible and realistic are the other two options. On the surface the claim that the burden is on the historian making a claim for or against a document appears reasonable. In fact, in much technical work this is the burden that is assumed by the investigator or scholar. If I claim an event is *authentic*, then I next have to try to make the case for it as a way of persuading the one who has questions or rejects the event. If I *doubt* the event, I have to assume the same type of argumentation to try to dissuade the person who claims the event took place. However, note what has subtly taken place. In effect, the document is back to having to prove its worth. *The advantage of this approach is that it is cautious in accepting historical claims. The danger is that singly-attested events risk getting slighted in the process of proving a document's worth.*

Others prefer to argue a document should be accepted for its testimony, unless it gives cause to doubt it. In popular parlance, it is "innocent until proven guilty." This slight shift in the burden suggests that documents should be given the right to speak and an initial benefit of the doubt – unless there is good reason to question their credibility. *The benefit of this approach is that single witnesses are given some role in the historical process. The danger is that the approach may be weak given the method of sorting out singly-attested claims.*

Discussing the problems the issue of burden of proof tries to face shows the dilemma of the historical task. The reality is that we work with partial knowledge concerning the events we investigate. Our sources are limited. Sources speak partially, even when they are accurate. They also speak from a perspective, as we noted in the previous section, making them inherently limited in their point of view. This is so, even when they are right about the facts they relate. Sources also only cover a portion of what actually took place. They are selective. Even the Bible makes this point. In John 21:25 we read, "But there are many other things Jesus did; if every one of them were written done, I suppose that the world itself could not contain the books that would be written." If we knew these other things, we would know more about the subject. We would be able to say more about those events and assess more about them. When people give respect to the testimony of Scripture and call it trustworthy, they are arguing that its testimony is sufficient to give us a meaningful understanding of God and his work. They are not arguing it tells us everything. It is one thing to be given enough to work adequately with a subject. This is what the Bible does.[25] It is another thing to argue the Bible tells us everything, which even the Bible itself makes clear it does not do. This is why the church has often argued that what we get in Scripture is sufficient for faith and practice. To speak *accurately* is not the same as speaking *exhaustively*.

So where does this leave us with the issue of burden of proof? I think we have to face the fact that we are caught practically somewhere between the options of giving the benefit of the doubt and having to show cause either for or against a document. On the one hand, it is best to give a document the opportunity to speak, especially if we know it is the only source we have. To do otherwise is in effect to rule it out. On the other, if there is not some standard of proof given for or against the document, then the door for specious claims is left open. What is interesting is that, practically, we often end up in the "proof" mode and not the "benefit of the doubt" mode anyway. Once someone challenges a document's claim, arguments must be summoned on its behalf to try to make the case to the one who has questions. However, note that in *raising* this challenge, one has moved *against* the document. The risk is that perfectly good testimony may be rejected simply because it is uncorroborated.

Certainly today the claims about the Bible's trustworthiness must be defended, for skeptics or doubters often raise objections of various levels of merit that require some response. The early church's apologists tended to assume this additional standard of burden in making their case for the credibility of events tied to their faith.

So are there tests one can apply to examine an event's or saying's trustworthiness? New Testament scholars often speak of these standards as the "criteria of authenticity," though they are aware of the limitations of the standards.[26] The first standard often noted is the criterion of *multiple attestation*. It looks for events or teaching that is multiply attested, that is, events that have more than one source strand that speak about them.[27] One can argue that the more independent the lines of tradition discuss the event and its details, the stronger the evidence for the event. The premise is that the event has left traces of its presence in distinct places, making its likelihood greater. The key here is the claim that a strand of tradition is *independent*, merely repeating an earlier reference to an event does not count. This standard is called multiple attestation.[28] For example, if one looks at Jesus' claim to be the Son of Man, a key claim about who he is, it is attested at every level of the gospel tradition, making its claims for authenticity strong.

A second standard is *dissimilarity*. It argues that if a teaching is unlike a person's cultural roots or unlike what came after the person, then it is likely to be authentic. It is the very uniqueness of the teaching that suggests someone else did not create it. This standard is of limited value, because it really highlights where one is unique and much of what happens in history is connected to a person's background, just as what emerges from a great figure often leaves an impact in kind. So very little actually emerges from this criterion. Jesus' *personal* use of the Semitic term *Abba*, referring to God as His own "Father" is often presented as fulfilling this criterion (e.g., Jesus speaks of "my Father in heaven"—we are not speaking merely about the use of the title Father for God). Jews rarely used "Father" as a title for God but did not do so in this individualized way. Such usage also was not present in the early church, though the general use of the title was. A variation of this standard is what has been called "double similarity and double dissimilarity."[29] Here the point is not that the teaching is unique, but that it is sufficiently different from both earlier and later practice and belief to be original. In a sense the example with *Abba* works here as well, since the use of *Abba* as a general title in Judaism and in the church is distinct enough in each of those settings not to match exactly Jesus' individualized use of the title. Son of Man also fits here, for the church almost never used the title independently. It is, except for one use, limited to Jesus' own speaking. Neither were elements of Jesus' use of the Son of Man as one who suffers like its use in Judaism. Nor does such a use of Son of Man appear outside the language of Jesus in the New Testament. Here is a "high" christological title affirming Jesus' unique authority whose presence is defensible as going back to him. We can be confident Jesus referred to himself in this way as God's authoritative representative.

A third standard is *coherence*. Anything that coheres with what the other standards suggest as authentic has good reason to be accepted. Thus, claims of authority that are similar to the way Jesus uses the title Son of Man become acceptable by this standard.[30]

Now many other textual details tend to be accepted not on the basis of such technical standards, but because they seem to cohere more generally with what we know about ancient history or the general portrait of the gospels. It is here that the argument becomes "we have no good reason to doubt this detail." Good historical work will defend a text at this more generic level as well. It argues that if we can make a coherent whole from the evidence a text gives us, then it has good reason to be accepted.[31]

Now all of these standards are often discussed with regard to the gospels, because gospel events are often multiply-attested. To use these standards is not to say they are perfect or foolproof, but they are a way to get into a discussion about how one can show trustworthiness. Many events about Jesus are defendable as trustworthy at this level. A collection of events made at this level gives us enough to work with that we can make firm statements about Jesus' message and self-understanding. The results are far more positive than anything the Jesus Seminar has argued.[32]

When it comes to singly-attested events, the work of making a case for a passage is more difficult. Here we are pretty much left to judgments about the general quality of the source giving the testimony at the places we can test it and to arguments from generic coherence with what we know from ancient culture or a composite understanding of the gospels. Still, even this little bit allows us to say some things about the solid quality of the biblical witness. It is also in this context that archaeology helps us. For it comes in and gives us a picture of the larger cultural realities into which the biblical portrait fits. This leads us into our next chapter, where we will trace how the findings of archaeology have often come in to add to our knowledge in such a way that what the Bible had singly-attested becomes generically multiply-attested, giving corroboration where it had been missing. In coming to this next chapter, we move from discussion of assumptions and method to looking at evidence.

LESSONS OF THE PAST:

What Archaeology Has Taught Us

Factor 5

For this unit I will concentrate mostly on the Old Testament, as most of the points we have covered up to now have related especially to the New Testament. It is here where corroborating the presence of events is hard. Most events are singly-attested and the distance of time traversed since their occurrence is great. It is here that archaeological work helps us gain perspective. Often what was claimed to be known by more skeptical readers of the Old Testament at the turn into the twentieth century has been shown to be suspect by the work of archaeologists. The discovery of additional sites and artifacts from the ancient world fills large gaps in our knowledge. Such discoveries often kill a hypothesis grounded only in a claim based on inferences. I will basically list a whole series of examples crossing the span of the Old Testament.[33]

✦ It was once claimed that the Hittites of the Old Testament were a mythic people. The reason was that no documents had been found naming them. But their reality was confirmed in 1906-12, when archaeologists found a Hittite legal code dating from 1300 BC and illuminating practices seen as far back as Genesis 23.

✦ It was argued that the presence of camels in Abraham's herds was an embellishment of later centuries. The reason was before 1950, camels were absent on any lists of livestock for the area. But discoveries in Sumerian texts that significantly predate Abraham and the surfacing of camel remains in 1955 and 1960 showed such a reference was possible.

✦ The sophistication of the priestly code as a developed practice was said to reflect a period far later than that of Moses. This led scholars to argue for a late P (priestly) document in the first five books of Moses. In 1901, the code of Hammurabi showed an extensive legal precedent for some of the legal issues raised in these Old Testament books. Subsequent discoveries in Egypt, Anatolia, Ugarit, and Emar show that Jewish practice was simple compared to the complex practices of their contemporary neighbors. Nothing about this code is out of step with what we know now about the culture of the period.

✦ In the nineteenth century it was popular to question the existence of the Assyrian Empire. In the Bible, Assyria conquered the ten Northern tribes of Israel in the eighth century BC. Early in the twentieth century, Sir Henry Layard found Nineveh, the Assyrian capital of what was clearly a powerful empire of its time.

✦ The art of writing was said to be late, not pre-dating the time of David and certainly too late to allow Moses to be an author of the first five Old Testament books. In the first decade of the twentieth century, the Gezar Calendar was found. It dated from 925 BC and was written in Hebrew. Then a huge collection of Ugaritic texts was found in 1929. They date from 1400 BC and are in a language more closely related to Hebrew than any other ancient language. Earlier discoveries at Ras Shamra revealed Phoenician writing in the 1500 BC period. Pots with writing on them in Palestine were found in 1958 and 1960. So the idea that writing was not possible for the period became discredited. In fact, just recently proto-Sinaitic inscriptions have been found dating back to 1900 BC, long before Moses.

✦ It was said that the description of temples with inner columns was not possible for Philistine temples like those involving Samson (1 Sam. 16). The argument was that these temples would be like Canaanite temples. At Tel Qasile and Tel Beit Shean, Philistine temples with inner columns were discovered and they were about two arms' lengths apart, like the scene described in the Samson text.[34]

✦ The idea of a David and a Davidic dynasty has been challenged as late as the 1990s. In 1995, an inscription at Tell Dan showed up with the letter *byt dwd*. The phrase means "house of David," confirming the existence of his royal line with him at its root.[35]

✦ The history of the conquest narratives have long been questioned, especially the accounts of Jericho, Ai, and Hazor. Though the site is still being worked as I write, Khirbet el-Makater may well be the ancient site of Ai.[36] A fortified city is there. It appears to have been destroyed at the time the Bible indicates. An ash level was found at Hazor that also corresponds to the biblical timing.

Now archaeology cannot prove that events took place, but what it can show is that details noted in events, some of them incidental, fit in the time and culture of the text. What it also shows is that we should be cautious commenting confidently about errors in the Bible merely because only the Bible attests to something. The unearthing of the right site may show that what we were working with was a very limited pool of knowledge. I turn to two examples from the New Testament.

✦ For a long time there was debate about the description in John 5:2 of a pool with five porticos in Jerusalem called variously Bethesda or Bethsaida. Many questioned its existence despite its wide attestation in ancient tradition because of its being characterized as a place where many gathered for healing. Different spellings of the locale in the New Testament manuscript tradition added to the tendency by many to reject the claim. In 1871 a French architect C. Mauss was restoring an old church and found a cistern 30 meters away. Later excavations in 1957-1962 clarified that it consisted of two large pools able to hold a large amount of water and people. Sometimes it takes years for a site to develop and reveal what it holds. Today virtually no one doubts the existence of this site.[37]

✦ I save for last in this section what is the most significant find of the last century for New Testament study.[38] It is the collection of texts found at Qumran near the Dead Sea in southern Israel in 1947. These texts were important because in New Testament study at that time it was often claimed that certain stories in the gospels betrayed a Hellenistic or Greek cultural setting, not the Jewish one in which Jesus worked. Thus, it was claimed where Hellenistic traces of expression could be found, it could be argued that these stories did not go back to Jesus, but were created by Gentiles in the early church.

All of those claims of evidence went out the window with Qumran.[39] For what was discovered was a host of texts from a Jewish separatist group that not only had severed relations with Gentiles, but with official Judaism. As separatists, they would not want to have anything to do with Hellenism. It was that association that was at the center of their protest and withdrawal to the desert to be a pure people. When these texts were unearthed and read, several of the so-called Hellenistic motifs (like the light-darkness dualistic contrast) showed up in their religious writing. All of a sudden what had been seen by many as evidence of exclusively Gentile ideas had shown up in a community that was exclusively Jewish. The texts confirmed how mixed the culture was when it came to the terminology of expressing religious hope.[40] The result has been an enhanced appreciation for the Jewishness of the gospel accounts and that the events tied to them fit nicely in that setting.

These many examples cannot prove the Bible's trustworthiness. What it does show, however, is the danger of being too quick to judge that if only the Bible says it, it is not true. It also suggests that again and again, the detail of the Bible fits into the cultural setting it describes. This enhances the case for the Bible's trustworthiness. Reasons for doubting it diminish.

Now we need to examine some actual examples of things people bring up to argue against the Bible's trustworthiness. A look at these specific examples will also help us understand what the Bible does and does not do when presenting events.

LESSONS FROM THE BIBLICAL TEXT:

Differences Often Reflect Differing Perspectives, Concerns, or More Literary Choices - Not Historical Error

Factor 6

We have already mentioned the approach that argues, in effect, difference = error. Now it is time to survey the array of forms in which such claims are made. We must examine some cases to see how wrong it is to jump to such a conclusion. As with the archaeology section, we will list the examples.

✦ A Peter Jennings ABC special on Jesus tried to play the infancy accounts of Matthew and Luke against each other to claim that Jesus was born in Nazareth, not Bethlehem.[41] The example is a good one to show how far some go to make their cases against Scripture, even when there is no solid evidence for the counter-claim. Luke explains how Joseph went to Bethlehem to register for a Roman census undertaken under Quirinius. He took Mary with him. Matthew simply tells the story of the birth in Bethlehem. Because Matthew lacked any account of how the couple got to Bethlehem, and Luke refers to a census that is otherwise unattested in Roman sources, the argument is that Jesus' birth in Bethlehem was a later creative detail made to have Jesus fulfill Scripture about where the Messiah would be born. It was alleged that the real Jesus was born in Nazareth, simply because he was called Jesus of Nazareth.

Numerous problems exist for such a view. I cover the example in some detail to show how complex some of these debates get.

There is no document that we have that makes a claim that Jesus was born in Nazareth. Thus, the alternative is proposed *without one piece of solid historical evidence.*

Using the name Jesus of Nazareth does not mean that he was born in Nazareth, but that he resided there for the bulk of his life. I regularly refer to myself as from Houston, because I grew up there from the age of five, even though I was born in Calgary, Canada. My friends would tell you I am a Houstonian in roots, not a Canadian. That is also how for years I have answered the question of where I am from.

Though there is no corroborative evidence for this census, the last section warned us about how cautious we should be to claim error for otherwise unattested events. Our pool of knowledge is not that complete. However, in the case of this census, Josephus notes a precedent-setting census under Quirinius, some ten years after Jesus was born (around AD 6). A challenge to the Lucan account, then, is the alleged inaccuracy of this detail. The Josephus parallel has often been used to argue that Luke has made a clear error. However, certain other features tell us to be cautious. We do know that Augustus did authorize many censuses—and it is likely we do not have a complete listing. We may also face the problem that a census begun under one governor may have been completed and made official under another, whose name became attached to it. This was not the age of e-mail. There also is some dispute about whether the text ties the time of Quirinius' rule to the time of the census, or simply references the fact that Quirinius was eventually governor and the census took place before that time.[42] Finally, there is the point that nothing about the timing of this detail actually refutes the locale of the birth. It only raises questions surrounding the circumstances of why Joseph is in Bethlehem. These factors suggest any claim of error is premature.[43]

One detail points to a Jewish aspect to this census that lends credibility to it. There was a precedent for taking a Jewish census in one's homeland from the Old Testament (2 Sam. 24). Such a detail explains why Joseph did not merely register in Galilee. If the Romans were to initiate a controversial census, it makes sense that they might try to soften the blow by doing it in a way that honored Jewish precedent.

All it would have taken to refute the "constructed locale" of the birth would have been the memory of any of those present when Jesus was really born in Nazareth. These villages were small enough that had Jesus been born in Nazareth, people would have known it and recognized the false claim of a Bethlehem birth. The gospels were written within a generation of the time of Jesus.[44] Such a false claim would have been easily refutable. Such a challenge was possible given the proximity of when the gospels were written to the events they describe.

We cover this example in some detail because it is one of the more difficult cases. It reveals the complexity of historical discussion. It also shows how when the Bible's credibility is questioned, *sometimes the alternative created has more problems than the biblical claim*. That is the case with this example. In fairness, the details of this example show why some texts raise questions. However, what often happens is that a debate over a detail is used to create an even less plausible hypothesis.

✦ Sometimes differences are the result of differing editorial choices on how much detail to present about an event and the literary perspective taken in telling it.[45] Such is the case with the healing of Jairus' daughter. In the Marcan and Lucan accounts, she dies about the time the woman with the hemorrhage is healed. In Matthew, she is dead before the healing begins. This difference of detail is one of literary choice. Matthew tells the account much more compactly. He has "telescoped" the story to keep it brief. Thus, his emphasis is on the fact that the daughter was dead by the time Jesus acted on her behalf. Mark and Luke have the full and precise detail. Such summarizing of the story is hardly to be considered error once we recognize how much briefer the Matthean account is.

✦ The example of who spoke to Jesus when the centurion's servant was healed is a famous case.[46] Did the centurion speak as Matthew's account portrays? Or did envoys representing him speak to Jesus and ask for the healing in his name? Ancient custom helps us here. In Israel, the idea of a "sent messenger" (*shaliach*) was viewed culturally as if the person himself was addressing you. The modern example is a politician's press spokes person. What is said is not important because of who one is, but because one is seen to speak for another. Again, *Luke has the detail right*, while *Matthew has simplified the account*, as he is prone to do as we saw in the previous example.

✦ What about differences of wording, especially in things Jesus said? Several points need attention here.[47] First, as a travelling preacher, Jesus would have said basic things many times in many different settings, any of which could have ended up in the memory of the tradition. So some "differences" may simply be variations resulting from repeated teaching recalled within the tradition in slightly diverse ways reflecting the distinct settings. Second, in the ancient world the responsibility was seen not in quotation, but in getting the gist of the teaching right.[48] This is technically known as the difference between the *vox* of Jesus (his voice) and the *verba* of Jesus (his words). Historical reliability requires only the accurate summarization of Jesus' teaching. Though citation is more precise, the use of accurate summary is still historical.

Again a modern example might suffice. When one listens to a five minute radio report today, sometimes the reporter uses an audio recording and cites the actual saying, while at other times she may report it and say, "President Reagan said today while speaking in New York that the communists must be stopped." Now let's assume you went and got a recording of that speech and that sentence in those words never actually appeared in the speech, but it was the "idea" of the speech. No one would complain that the summary was untrustworthy. They would immediately appreciate the fact that a thirty minute speech had been reduced to its core idea so it could be told in one sentence. Ancient writing operates at this level.

We can see this approach to verbal speech by looking at specific examples in the text that we know belong to the same setting. For example, did the voice form heaven at Jesus' baptism say, "THIS is my beloved Son" (Matthew 3:17) or "YOU are my beloved Son" (Mark 1:11; Luke 3:22)? We cannot be sure, because both versions are reported, though the likelihood is that Matthew has again made a summarizing and explanatory change as he often does. Nonetheless, the difference does not alter the gist of the story, that a voice from heaven endorsed Jesus as his unique Son at this event. Or take what Peter actually confessed Jesus to be at Caesarea Philippi. Was it, "You are the Messiah" (Mark 8:29), "The Messiah of God" (Luke 9:20), or "You are the Messiah, the Son of the Living God" (Matthew 16:16)? As is often the case, there is slight variation, but the gist is the same.

Another example is the word of the centurion at the cross. Did he say as Mark 15:39

reports, "Surely this man was the Son of God?" Or was it as Luke 23:49 has it, "Certainly this man was innocent?" One solution here would be that each gospel writer chose what the centurion said, assuming that the centurion simply made both statements. But it is also likely that Luke took the confession and brought out its import – namely, the centurion recognized that Jesus was innocent of the charges he was just executed for (and so he was God's Son). In other words, Luke, who highlights Jesus' innocence as he recounts the Roman and Jewish leaders' trial examination scenes in Luke 23, closes with the focus on Jesus' innocence, an innocence that also means he was the Son he claimed to be. The alteration allows the gospel writer to highlight the presentation of a genuine historical implication in the intent of the saying.

The claim that the Bible is trustworthy operates within a standard of credibility that recognizes that these texts have these kinds of variation and choice in them.

✦ The difference in the order of the temptation, already noted above, also makes a point about arrangement. In Matthew 4:1-11 the order of the temptation is (1) turn bread to stone, (2) cast yourself down from the temple, and (3) call to worship Satan. In Luke 4:1-13 the second and third temptations are reversed. Someone rearranged the order. In this case, Luke is the one most often suggested. Jerusalem plays a key role in his narrative; so he is believed to have highlighted that temptation by placing it last as a particularly significant one. Here topical and thematic concerns have led to a difference. However, again, the gist of the account is not compromised by the move. One author simply did not care what was the order of the three temptations, but simply what they were. Mark was even simpler, only naming that fact that Jesus was tempted with no details.

✦ A final example is the difference in the responses of the disciples when Jesus walks on the water in Matthew 14:33 and Mark 6:52. In Matthew the event leads to a confession of Jesus as "Son of God" while Mark ends with a note about how the disciples failed to understand. The difference here is fueled by two elements. First, Mark is interested in explaining how their lack of understanding *during* the event was related to their failure to connect the significance of the miracle of the loaves to Jesus' ability to walk on the water. The earlier event had failed to be adequately grasped to make this event understandable. In addition, Mark often points out quite directly the disciples' shortcomings. On the other hand, Matthew highlights the *result* of this event and its impact on the disciples' understanding *after* this event. Thus, this example reaffirms our earlier remarks about how different perspectives on an event make for different but complementary emphases.

Such examples could be multiplied. The point of them is that difference ≠ error. Often other factors explain plausibly the reason for the difference. Some hard cases do exist, but in general, it can be said that the Bible has a solid claim to being trustworthy in how it presents the core elements of its accounts. The result is that the Bible's credibility is sustainable.

LESSONS FROM THE BIBLICAL TEXT:

The Bible's Claim for Miracles Are Plausible When One Considers the Response to Exodus and Resurrection Claims

Factor 7

For a modern person, one of the greatest hurdles to accepting the Bible's reliability is the presence of miracles throughout its account.[49] I will not tackle this question philosophically,[50] other than to note that once one believes a personal God exists, then the logical possibility that he acts in his creation opens up. One can get lost in these abstract worldview debates, important as they are. Sometimes they can turn into a "he said, she said" debate with atheists and agnostics on one side and theists on the other. No doubt here is a case where one's particular worldview impacts how one reads the Bible's claims for miracles. In fact, even to call such events "supernatural" virtually accepts that it is the natural world that we are so used to. Miracles were never described using this term in the Bible. Rather terms like "powers," "signs," or "wonders" were used to make the point that God was marvelously at work in such acts. For God to act in this way was not a suspension of natural law, but rather a result of his more directly involving himself in his creation. Such serious objections to the Bible's credibility have been honestly faced and rebutted, as the noted works treat this question in appropriate detail.[51]

Is there other evidence for taking this claim seriously that God has acted so directly? Rather than leaving ourselves to arguments often constructed out of existing worldview commitments, what might history have to say?

We start with the account of the origin of Israel as a nation. What caused a people to be formed and to be drawn together, willing to live their lives with distinct practices and a unique monotheistic faith in comparison to their neighbors? The exodus accounts explain the move to the promised land as part of a series of great, direct acts by God on behalf of Israel, including acts of revelation and judgment, the ten plagues and the crossing of the Sea. Though one could place the credit at the feet of a great man like Moses, it is difficult to accept the effect of the creation of a nation out of bondage through the mere natural acts of one man. What led him to take charge in the way he did?

Strict history can only confirm that Israel emerged out of obscurity to become a national force in Palestine. The biblical account claims that the liberation of Israelites out of slavery and from the hands of Egypt had a miraculous dimension to it. We cannot "instant replay" the events to see if the miracles actually took place. What we can see is the impact of the belief that they took place.[52] When miracles happen, they leave a wake of results as their effect. Though it is true that other cultures also have made claims about divine intervention lying at the roots of their existence, it is the staying power and uniqueness of Israel's existence that suggests that what took place made a deep impression on her people.[53] Something profound made them different.

The resurrection is a similar situation. Here we have the advantage of events that are recorded within the lifetime of several of those who claimed to have the experience. Perhaps the greatest evidence for the resurrection is again seen in the change and reaction of those who claimed to experience it. Disciples, who openly admit in their community documents that they came to the task with no formal training and with a long period of shocking ineptness in responding to Jesus, become courageous leaders. They stand firm in the face of the threat of death and rejection by the Jewish leaders who resist them. This did not involve one or two people, but a whole host of leaders who left their mark on history.

The most outstanding example in this category of people was the former chief persecutor of the church, Paul. What caused Paul to be transformed from hostile to apostle? His own testimony is that he had an encounter with the risen Jesus (Acts 9). Both he and Peter, along with others like the Lord's brother James, died for this belief.[54] They were convinced that the tomb in Jerusalem had been emptied of Jesus' body by the power of God. No historical theory adequately explains this transformation and the depth of this conviction as well as the idea that a resurrection, a miracle of the highest order, took place. The accounts on the resurrection are filled with the quite natural, initial response of disciples that the first claims of resurrection were not well received. The gospels indicate that the resurrection was not embraced as a given when it took place (Matthew 28; Mark 16; Luke 24; John 20). Most of the disciples reacted much as a modern person might to the initial news. Yet the conviction came to be established that this was the only credible explanation for the empty tomb and for the *mass* transformation of a host of inept disciples into convinced believers. Jesus was now raised and was still alive. Something about the promise of everlasting life and an encounter with the risen Jesus led the disciples to be willing to face death. At the core of Christian belief stand these crucial issues tied to life, death, and God. Also at the historical core of the faith stand the powerful claims and reality of the disciples' transformation.

This historical core to the Christian faith argues that God's power in miracle and over life comes together in the historical reality of resurrection. The resurrection, then, vividly illustrates how God has power over creation and life in a way that makes him able to give everlasting life. This decisive act of God casts its confirming shadow over the biblical claim that God has been active in history throughout the story its accounts narrate. Resurrection not only points to the reality of miracle, but to a vindication of Jesus and his claims that makes this raised one the center of God's divine activity. All of this evidence adds to the biblical claim for the Bible's credibility. It also explains the call to faith in Jesus that the Bible makes.

CONCLUSION

The Bible Is Trustworthy

Assessing historical claims for any ancient document is difficult work. No one today can interview the witnesses. There are no video tapes. There is no DNA evidence to find. There is no way to go back and recreate the events and check them out. What we do have is a portrait of a people and their religious beliefs. As they tell their story, we can see if the accounts connect to the culture they describe. On this point archaeology tells us the Bible has a good record of credibility. We can ask if the history of the texts' recording is credible, so that we can be sure what we have in the texts was what was written. The Bible's record here is outstanding. The New Testament is the most widely attested ancient text humanity possesses. We can ask about the quality of the sources used and the history of the way in which tradition operated. Here again we encounter works, in the case of the New Testament, written within a generation or so of the events. These sources are rooted in eyewitness testimony coming from people who regard telling the truth as a moral imperative. The accounts operate within an oral tradition culture that has shown itself to be very careful in how it preserves the gist of the story. Finally, we have the effect on peoples' lives at the time these works were written. The transformation that the message in the Bible brought to those who experienced the events is compelling testimony to its veracity. It was enough to cause people to leave everything and risk everything, including their lives, for what was taught. In sum, the Bible is historically trustworthy.

The case is strongest where it matters most—in its portrayal of Jesus. This is why we have concentrated on the New Testament and the gospels. Strong historical support exists for a credible portrait of Jesus, despite loud claims otherwise often surfacing in the media. The biblical material points to a figure who challenged the religious leadership of Judaism and who made claims to be a uniquely-sent representative of God. He brought to realization promises made long ago.

In a booklet this size we cannot make the case for trustworthiness passage by passage, but we can show in general terms why the objections more skeptical people raise in comparing biblical differences are not ultimately persuasive. That is what we have tried to do. Other resources go text by text. What we have shown is that when one reads the Bible, one is encountering a claim that God has spoken in these texts. God was powerfully active in the events the Bible describes.

The Bible is not a book like any other. It makes a claim that God spoke and speaks through its message. It argues that as his creatures, we are accountable to him for what he has revealed. The trustworthiness of Scripture points to its authority as well. Scripture is far more than a history book, as good and trustworthy as that history is. It is a book that calls on us to examine our lives and relationship to God. Beyond the fascinating history, it contains vital and life-transforming truths about God and us. It is worth reading, studying, and pondering for reasons that extend far beyond the history it so faithfully records.

ENDNOTES

[1] This point was made years ago by Manchester scholar, F. F. Bruce in his book, *The New Testament Documents: Are They Reliable?* 5th ed. (Downers Grove, IL: Inter Varsity Press, 1960).

[2] For a helpful overview discussion, see Donald Guthrie, "Canon of the New Testament," in *the Zondervan Pictorial Encyclopedia of the Bible*, ed. Merrill Tenney (Grand Rapids: Zondervan, 1975), vol. 1, pp. 731-45, as well as Bruce, *New Testament Documents*, pp. 21-28.

[3] The prophets appears to include Joshua, Judges-Ruth, Samuel, Kings, Chronicles, Ezra-Nehemiah, Esther, Isaiah, Jeremiah-Lamentations, Ezekiel, Daniel, the twelve minor prophets, and (perhaps) Song of Solomon.

[4] For this discussion on Old Testament canon including issues tied to the apocryphal books, see Gleason Archer, *A Survey of Old Testament Introduction* (Chicago: Moody Press, 1964), pp. 68-76.

[5] *Against the Heresies* 3.11.8.

[6] Eusebius, *Ecclesiastical History* 3.39.15; Irenaeus, *Against the Heresies* 3.1.2.

[7] For the Fathers, see the Loeb Classical Library's two volumes, *The Apostolic Fathers,* edited by Kirsopp Lake.

[8] For a detailed discussion of these key verses, Darrell L. Bock, *Luke 1:1—9:50*. BECNT 3a (Grand Rapids: Baker, 1994), pp. 51-67.

[9] For these verses, Leon Morris, *The Gospel According to John,* rev. ed. (Grand Rapids: Wm. B. Eerdmans, pp. 776-77.

[10] For a philosophical defense of the position arguing for a harmony between the divine and human roles in biblical texts, see William Lane Craig, "'Men Moved

by the Holy Spirit Spoke from God' 2 Peter 1:21: A Middle Knowledge Perspective on Biblical Inspiration," *Philosophia Christi*, Series 2, 1 (1999): 45-82.

[11] For the details on these issues, Donald Guthrie, *New Testament Introduction*. 4th rev. ed. (Downers Grove: InterVarsity Press, 1990).

[12] For these issues, Darrell L. Bock, "The Words of Jesus: Live, Jive, or Memorex," in Michael Wilkens and J. P. Moreland, ed., *Jesus Under Fire*. (Grand Rapids: Zondervan, 1995), pp. 73-99, esp. 78-81. For the stability of Jewish oral tradition, Rainer Riesner, "Jesus as Preacher and Teacher," *Jesus and the Oral Gospel Tradition*. JSNTMS 64, ed. Henry Wansbrough (Sheffield: Sheffield Academic Press, 1991), pp. 185-210. The discussion has roots in what has been called the "Scandinavian school" of New Testament studies and is associated with the work of Harold Riesenfeld and Birger Gerhardsson. See especially Gerhardsson's *Memory and Manuscript: Oral Tradition and Written Transmission in Rabbinic Judaism and Early Christianity* (Lund: Gleerup, 1961). The key chapters in this work are chapters 10-11.

[13] R. Laird Harris, "The Dead Sea Scrolls and the Old Testament Text," in *New Perspectives on the Old Testament*, ed. J. Barton Payne (Waco: Word, 1970), pp. 201-11.

[14] This is one of the basic points in Bruce's study on the reliability of the New Testament as cited in n. 1. See pp. 10-20.

[15] Kurt and Barbara Aland, *The Text of the New Testament: An Introduction to the Critical Editions and to the Theory and Practice of Modern Textual Criticism*, trans. E. F. Rhodes (Grand Rapids: Eerdmans; Leiden: E. J. Brill, 1987) and Paul D. Wegner, *The Journey from Texts to Translations* (Grand Rapids: Baker, 1999), p. 235.

[16] C. Stephen Evans, *The Historical Jesus and the Jesus of Faith: The Incarnational Narrative as History* (Oxford: Clarendon Press, 1996), discusses the philo-

sophical roots of the various views that the third factor of our booklet raises. For a treatment of the three categories of positiviism, phenomenalism, and critical realism, see N. T. Wright, *The New Testament and the People of God* (Minneapolis: Fortress Press, 1992), pp. 31-37.

[17] On critical realism, Ben F. Meyer, *Reality and Illusion in New Testament Scholarship: A Primer in Critical Realist Hermeneutics* (Collegeville, MN: The Liturgical Press, 1994), esp. pp. 59-113.

[18] The Roman example noted was highlighted in a recent prime time special on Jesus as an explanation of the parallel between Jesus and the Roman ruler. For a full discussion of these issues, see the classic work by J. Gresham Machen, *The Virgin Birth of Christ* (New York: Harper & Row, 1930), especially pp. 317-79.

[19] By parallel accounts, we mean passages in different gospels that share a description of the same event. Thus the accounts "parallel" each other in terms of the event portrayed, even if their details differ.

[20] Darrell L. Bock, *Blasphemy and Exaltation in Judaism* (Grand Rapids: Baker, 2000). This same volume appeared earlier in the *Wissenschaftliche Untersuchungen zum Neuen Testament* series 2 out of Tübingen in Germany, one of the most prestigious New Testament monograph series in the world. I note this to show how monographs arguing for the credibility of the Bible have appeared at the most technical levels of New Testament study. This volume details the case for this scene's credibility. It goes without saying that if this scene is credible, and a strong case can be made for it, then we know an awful lot about what Jesus claimed for himself.

[21] The Jewish works involved here are the second century BC *Exagoge of Ezekiel* and *1 Enoch.* In *Exagoge,* Moses has a dream in which he sits on God's throne in heaven as events of the Exodus take place. This explains Exodus 7:1, where the Bible says that Moses "will be God to Pharaoh." In *1 Enoch,* a figure called Son of

Man and later identified as Enoch exercises full judgment authority from heaven as God's right hand assistant. These texts show that bridges to what Jesus expressed existed in Judaism already, even though Jesus' claims are expressed even more emphatically and directly. Here is an example where texts outside the Bible help us appreciate what is in the Bible better, reinforcing the point made above that additional sources can help open up our perspective on events the Bible treats.

[22] For this section, see Stewart C. Goetz and Craig Blomberg, "The Burden of Proof," *Journal for the Study of the New Testament* 11 (1981):39-63; R. T. France, *Jesus and the Old Testament* (London: Tyndale, 1971), pp. 15-24.

[23] For example, we would know little about Livy or the early history of the Franks if we applied this standard outside Scripture. G. J. Reneir, *History: Its Purpose and Method* (London: George Allen & Unwin, 1950), pp. 90-91. Of the 142 books of Livy's *Roman History*, only 35 survive. Some of what we know about Rome only goes back to one source.

[24] For a solid treatment of ancient historiography, Charles Fornara, *The Nature of History in Ancient Greece and Rome* (Berkeley: University of California Press, 1983).

[25] 2 Timothy 3:16-17 promises that Scripture "is profitable for teaching, for reproof, for correction, and for training in righteousness, that the man of God may be complete, equipped for every good work."

[26] Robert H. Stein, "The 'Criteria' for Authenticity," in *Gospel Perspectives, Volume I*, ed. R. T. France and David Wenham (Sheffield: Sheffield Academic Press, 1980), pp. 225-63; Stanley Porter, *The Criteria for Authenticity in Historical-Jesus Research: Previous Discussion and New Proposals. Journal for the Study of the New Testament* Supplement Series 191 (Sheffield: Sheffield Academic Press, 2000).

[27] A variation on this is to look for teaching that shows up in multiple forms (or genre types) of stories.

Thus if teaching is in a miracle account and in a parable, the likelihood for its authenticity is strengthened.

[28] Often the source units are seen as Marcan, teaching shared by Matthew and Luke (often called Q), uniquely Matthean (M), and uniquely Lucan (L) strands.

[29] The Jesus scholar N. T. Wright is responsible for this criterion in his *Jesus and the Victory of God* (Minneapolis: Fortress, 1996), p. 86.

[30] Other criteria exist, such as appeals to a Palestinian setting or looking for Aramaisms in the tradition, which point to an early origin for the tradition. (Aramaic was the Semitic dialect often spoken in first century Palestine) However, the three we mention are the most discussed. Stein's article as cited in note 26 above covers all the proposals.

[31] N. T. Wright's study of Jesus often appeals to this more synthetic and holistic type of argument.

[32] The Institute for Biblical Research, a professional society of evangelical biblical scholars, is in the midst of an ongoing project where those who have engaged in technical Jesus studies have isolated ten key events in the life of Jesus they believe can be defended at this technical level. These events can then serve as the base for appealing to the coherence of much of what we see in the gospels. The results are to appear annually in the *Bulletin for Biblical Research* starting with volume 10 until the project is completed. This periodical is produced by the *Institute for Biblical Research,* a society of evangelical scholars who teach Old and New Testament. To obtain this periodical and subsequent editions, contact the *Institute for Biblical Research,* P.O. Box 275, Winona Lake, IN 46590-0275.

[33] The first five examples noted below are found in Gleason Archer, *A Survey of Old Testament Introduction*, especially pp. 163-76. All details on these five examples can be found within these pages.

[34] Neal Bierling, *Giving Goliath His Due: New Archaeological Light on the Philistines* (Grand Rapids:

Baker Book House, 1992), p. 115; Trude Dothan, *People of the Sea: The Search for the Philistines* (New York: Macmillan, 1992); Amihai Mazar, *Excavations at Tell Qasile. Parrt 1. QEDEM 12* (Jerusalem: Hebrew University, 1980). My thanks for the next three illustrations go to Rick Hess, Professor of Old Testament at Denver Seminary and to Gordon Johnston, Professor of Old Testament at Dallas Theological Seminary.

[35] Avraham Biran, *Biblical Dan* (Jerusalem: Israel Exploration Society), p. 275-277; Avraham Biran and Joseph Naveh, "An Aramaic Stele Fragment from Tel Dan", *Israel Exploration Journal* 42, no 2-3, p. 81-86; Avraham Biran and Joseph Naveh, "The Tel Dan Inscription: A New Fragment," *Israel Exploration Journal* 45, no. 1, pp. 1-8. Some have challenged this reading, but the rebuttal in support of it has been strong and is convincing. See Anson Rainey, "The 'House of David' and the House of the Deconstructionists," *Biblical Archaeology Review* 20 (Nov/Dec 1994): 47; David Noel Freedman and Jeffrey C. Geoghegan, "House of David Is There!" *Biblical Archaeology Review* (March/April 1995): 78-79; and K. A. Kitchen, "A Possible Mention of David in the Late Tenth Century BCE and Deity God as Dead as the Dodo?" *Journal for the Study of the Old Testament* 76 (1997): 29-44.

[36] David Livingston, "Location of Bethel and Ai Reconsidered," *Westminster Theological Journal* 33 (1970): 20-44; *idem,* "Traditional Site of Bethel Questioned," *Westminster Theological Journal* 34 (1971): 39-50; *idem*, "Further Considerations on the Location of Bethel at el-Bireh," *Palestinian Exploration Journal* 126 (1994): 154-59; on Jericho, Bryant G. Wood, "Did the Israelites Conquer Jericho?" *Biblical Archaeological Review* 162 (1990): 44-58.

[37] This example, along with many details on other New Testament sites can be found in Jack Finegan, *The Archaeology of the New Testament: The Life of Jesus and the Beginning of the Church*, rev ed. (Princeton:

Princeton University Press, 1992). The example is treated on pp. 226-232.

[38] Other examples for the New Testament can be found in Bruce, *The New Testament Documents: Are They Reliable?* pp. 80-99. Among the examples he discusses are the discovery of the pool of Bethesda that fits the description in John's gospel (John 5:2) and the finding of an inscription for the Temple telling foreigners to keep out of the sacred precincts.

[39] That this debate still exists is indicated in Donald Guthrie, *New Testament Introduction,* rev. ed. (Downers Grove, IL:Inter-Varsity, 1970), pp. 277-79. Despite the continuing debate, what Qumran did was show indisputably that Jewish thinking could go in such directions.

[40] The mixed nature of first century culture is developed in detail by Martin Hengel, *Judaism and Hellenism: Studies in their Encounter in Palestine in the Early Hellenistic Period* (Philadelphia: Fortress, 1974).

[41] This show aired to an estimated 16 million viewers on 26 June 2000. A PBS special on Jesus two years earlier called *From Jesus to Christ* made similar claims.

[42] For a detailed discussion of the options, Darrell L. Bock, *Luke 1:1—9:50*, pp. 903-09.

[43] This is true especially in light of the fact that Luke is widely regarded as a meticulous and accurate ancient historian. See Colin Hemer, *The Book of Acts in the Setting of Hellenistic History* (Tübingen: Mohr/Siebeck, 1989).

[44] Even if one dates Matthew after AD 70, this point is true, though most conservatives place all the synoptics before AD 70 or within a few years of it. For issues tied to dating of the gospels, see Donald Guthrie, *New Testament Introduction*, 4th rev. ed. pp. 53-56 (Matthew), 84-89 (Mark), 125-131 (Luke), and 297-303 (John).

[45] For the explanation of this example and many others, Craig Blomberg, *The Historical Reliability of the Gospels* (Downers Grove, IL: InterVarsity Press, 1987). For this specific example, see p. 135.

[46] Blomberg, *Historical Reliability*, p. 134.

[47] This issue is considered in detail in my "The Words of Jesus: Live, Jive or Memorex?" in *Jesus under Fire*, eds. Michael Wilkins and J. P. Moreland (Grand Rapids: Zondervan, 1995), pp. 73-99.

[48] A famous citation in the *History of the Peloponnesian War* of Thucydides makes this point (1.22.1), when he claims in rendering the speeches that he has not been exact, not recalling the exact substance of the speech nor have his witnesses, but he has "kept as close as possible to the total opinion expressed by the actual words."

[49] A famous liberal New Testament scholar, Rudolf Bultmann said it this way, "Man's knowledge and mastery of the world have advanced to such an extent through science and technology that it is no longer possible for anyone seriously to hold the New Testament view of the world." He went on to say one cannot believe in the electric light bulb *and* miracles. "New Testament and Mythology," in *Kerygma and Myth*, ed. H. W Bartsch (London: SPCK, 1953), pp. 4-7.

[50] See R. Douglas Geivett and Gary Habermas, ed., *In Defense of Miracles* (Downers Grove, IL: InterVarsity Press, 1997).

[51] For more discussion of the so-called scientific, philosophical and historical objections to miracles, Blomberg, *Historical Reliability*, pp. 73-80. Also Colin Brown, *Miracles and the Critical Mind* (Grand Rapids: Eerdmans, 1984); Graham H. Twelftree, *Jesus the Miracle Worker: A Historical and Theological Study* (Downers Grove, IL: InterVarsity Press, 1999). He engages the discussion at all these levels including a detailed treatment of each miracle account. A classic study is by the ex-Oxford don, C. S. Lewis, *Miracles* (London: Collins, 1960).

[52] See Kevin Miller, "Did the Exodus Never Happen?" *Christianity Today* (7 September 1998): 44ff., which argues for a plausible historical context for this event.

[53] A closer look at these alleged parallels also shows that the comparison is often superficial. This is especially true in the case of comparing the miracle accounts about Jesus with other such accounts, Blomberg, *Historical Reliability*, pp. 80-92. Greco-Roman accounts have a physicality to them that the Jesus accounts lack. Thus, men speak with animals or birds, transform themselves into other creatures, engage in acts of magical "charm," or appear in two places at once. The Jesus accounts have none of this. Another important point to note is that some of the closer parallels adduced to Jesus actually post-date his time so that there was no cultural influence moving the gospel writers to create stories like the Greeks (e.g., Apollonius who was said to raise people from the dead). Some scholars have argued that what the Greco-Roman parallels did was make Jews even more resistant to making such "divine" comparisons; Carl Holladay, *Theios Anêr in Hellenistic Judaism* (Missoula: Scholars Press, 1977).

[54] For the tradition associated with the deaths of Paul and Peter, see the fourth-century early church historian Eusebius, *Ecclesiastical History* 2.25. For the death of James, see the first century Jewish historian Josephus, *Antiquities* 20.200-203.

RECOMMENDATIONS FOR FURTHER SUGGESTED READING

Blomberg, Craig. *The Historical Reliability of the Gospels.* Downers Grove, IL: InterVarsity Press, 1987. A careful consideration of all aspects of the question of the historical trustworthiness of the gospels.

Bruce, F F. *The New Testament Documents: Are They Reliable?* Grand Rapids: Eerdmans, 1960. This work treats the question of the roots of the New Testament biblical tradition in detail.

Graham H. Twelftree, *Jesus the Miracle Worker.* Downers Grove, IL: InterVarsity Press, 1999. A comprehensive study of the miracle accounts of the New Testament.

Sheldon, Jeffery L., *Is the Bible True?* Grand Rapids/San Francisco: Zondervan/HarperSF, 1999. A treatment of the Bible's general reliability in light of archaeological discoveries and historical and textual research.

Wilkins, Michael and J. P. Moreland, ed. *Jesus Under Fire.* Grand Rapids: Zondervan, 1995. A treatment and critical analysis of how more skeptical readings of the historical Jesus (e.g., the Jesus Seminar) inadequately treat the history about him.

PROJECTED BOOKLETS IN THE RZIM CRITICAL QUESTIONS SERIES

William Craig, *God, Are You There? Five Reasons God Exists and Three Reasons It Makes a Difference* (available)

Paul Copan, *Is Everything Really Relative? Examining the Assumptions of Relativism and the Culture of* Truth *Decay* (available)

Scott Armstrong, *Who's Shaping My Life? Assessing the Media's Influence on Our Culture*

Darrell Bock, *Can I Trust the Bible? Defending the Bible's Reliability* (available)

David K. Clark and James Beilby, *Why Bother With Truth? Arriving at Knowledge in a Skeptical Society* (available)

Douglas Geivett, *Can a Good God Allow Evil? Making Sense of Suffering*

Klaus Issler, *What Does It Mean To Be Human? Understanding Who We Really Are*

Mark Linville, *Is Everything Permitted? Moral Values in a World without God* (available)

L. T. Jeyachandran *Does the East Have the Answers? Getting Perspective on Eastern Religion and Philosophy*

Stuart McAllister, *Born to Shop? Exposing the Threat of a Consumer Culture*

Paul K. Moser, *Why Doesn't God Make Himself More Obvious? Understanding the God Who Hides and Seeks* (available)

Michael Ramsden, *What's the Point? Finding Meaning and Hope in God*

John Mark Reynolds, *Do the Bible and Science Conflict? Reconciling the Differences*

Ravi Zacharias, *What's So Special About Jesus? Encountering Christ Among the World's Religions*

Keith Pavlischek, *Should God Be Excluded from the Public Square? Undestanding the Role of Faith in the Public Life*

Charles Taliaferro, *Is The Idea of God Coherent? Making Sense of the Divine Attributes*

Paul Chamberlain, *Whose Life is it Anyway? Assessing Physician-Assisted Suicide*

Christopher Wright, *Isn't the God of the Bible Cruel and Vindictive? Understanding Ethical Issues in the Bible*

William Lane Craig, *What Does God Know? Reconciling Divine Foreknowledge and Human Freedom*

J.P. Moreland, *Does the Soul Exist? Recovering the Soul in the Philosophy of Mind*

If you have further questions or are in need of additional resources, please contact

**Ravi Zacharias International Ministries,
4725 Peachtree Corners Circle, Suite 250,
Norcross, Georgia, USA 30092.**

Website: www.rzim.org
Phone: 800.448.6766
Fax: 770.729.1729
E-mail: rzim@rzim.org

Regional Offices

Canada office
2476 Argentia Road ❧ Suite 203 Mississauga,
Ontario L5N 6M1 Canada

European office
97A St. Aldate's,
Oxford ❧ OX1 1BT ❧ United Kingdom

India office
Plot No. 211 & 212
V.G.P. Nagar ❧ Mogappair West,
Chennai 600 058

Singapore office
c/o International Christian Mission
9 Francis Thomas Drive
Singapore ❧ 359336

RZIM is a ministry founded by Dr. Ravi Zacharias with the goal to reach and challenge those who shape the ideas of a culture with the credibility of the message of Jesus Christ.

If you are interested in obtaining a first-rate philosophical journal featuring articles written by leading Christian philosophers, we encourage you to subscribe to *Philosophia Christi*, the journal of the Evangelical Philosophical Society (EPS). Please contact:

Paul Pardi
35706 25th Pl. South
Federal Way, WA 98003
eps8451@epsociety.org

Published by RZIM
Ravi Zacharias International Ministries
4725 Peachtree Corners Circle, Suite 250
Norcross, Georgia 30092
www.rzim.org

Library of Congress Cataloging-in-Publication Data
Bock, Darrell L., 2001
Can I Trust the Bible?
ISBN 1-930107-03-X

1.Bible - Antiquities 2. Jesus Christ - Historicity
3.Christianity-Philosophy.

1-030101 - 5000